SKILLS

SKILLS

Dr. Rabindranath Athri

PARTRIDGE
A Penguin Random House Company

To order additional copies of this book, contact
Partridge India
000 800 10062 62
orders.india@partridgepublishing.com

www.partridgepublishing.com/india

CONTENTS

JUST

YOU

&

ME

ATHRI

SOFTSKILLS INITIATIVE

ESTD.1994

COCHIN-682020

Athri was fortunate to attend a five day workshop on NLP by one of the founders of NLP, Mr. Richard Bandler. That was the decisive moment when Athri got obsessed with training. His background from 1967 to 1997, as a Medical Representative, Field Manager and Area Manager, gave him just the right climate and atmosphere for training. In this MNC Pharma Company in which he worked, (John Wyeth and brother limited) the emphasis and practice of training was practically a day and night affair.

The area managers go to the HO (Bombay) every month and literally mug up word to word detail, the specific technical words, the sequence of the sentences, the display of the folder, the eye contact, the closing with pointed statements in order to get assurance of prescription from the doctor, was all practice so thoroughly that this extremely content and process specific detail is ground very thoroughly at the field managers meetings and then on to the medical representatives meeting. This cyclic intensive training literally got into Athri's psyche.

This was not all. While working with the representatives every doctor call is deeply analyzed with regard to the objective, strategy, convincing technique timely display of the display material, mentally noting down the yes signals and closing was diligently done at every call.

Soft Skills Initiatives is a natural evolution as far as Athri is concerned.

Before Pharma experience Athri had the privilege of working in Avery India Madras. He worked as GM in 3 auto dealerships (Daewoo, Hyundai, and Tata Motors). He moved to ICFAI as Consultant trainer (soft skills). He worked as Marketing Manger in SD Pharmacy and GM in two Pan India Training Companies. He also worked as Marketing Manager (Overseas customers) and growing software developer and for a short while for ICICI home Loans.

This rich and varied experience helped him establish himself as a note worthy and successful trainer all over South India.

The title of the booklet wants to convey to the reader

JUST

We are aware our readers are always in a hurry. They are in the mobile Era. So if I say **just**, they are likely to perceive that this booklet is meant to be short, crisp, yet with a worthwhile content.

YOU

We are presently living in an I, Me, My mind set.

Our Sanskrit heritage tells us of **PRATHAMAPURUSAHA** and this important person is the second person in our commonly understood 1st, 2nd and 3rd person. So the importance is given to **prathamapurusha,** the second person so that in our relationships we give emphasis an importance only to second person. The advantage in this is in relationships, self awareness, empathy, team dynamics, leadership etc.

That is why **YOU**

ME

When I understand you and the many people around me I get to understand THE ME.

When I understand **the me**, obviously my self awareness is enhanced.

I know my strengths, my potential, my ambitions, my setbacks, my response and practically all that I need to go where I want to go.

INTRODUCTION

I am very conscious that I am addressing the most important segment of our society today. Obviously in the present scenario, the youngsters of India have started taking charge of their own lives and this is something that is very evident.

50% of India's population consist of youngsters who are below 25 years. This is a huge demographic advantage for us inIndia. This advantage will surely take India forward, seeing successful young entrepreneurs with a vision so typical of them.

People born before 1947, in thepre-independence era unfortunately did not think or do much for themselves and to some extent were under the influence of the British mindset. Over a period of 2 decades after1947 this mindset has changed and youngsters born in the 70's has a powerful positive mindset. This change along with the demographic advantage is a turning point in the great history of India. It is said that the soft skill awareness in India is only 3% where as that inPhilippines or Singapore is as high as 61% & 53%.

This asset makes the Philippines very much high indemand in terms ofcustomer centric jobs all over the world. Nowadays we often find Philippine girls doing customer centric jobs in huge shopping malls, in nursing professions and in the hospitality sector. As youngsters in need of employability skills, we surely have a lot to learn from them. Acquiring soft skillsis not somekind of rocket science. However they can be learnt just like one learns language skills. What is important is that just learning these skills is no use. The coach should be able to demonstrate and repeatedly show youngsters the implementation of these skills with thorough role play, workshop and repeat performances which in a matter of a week should bring about correction.

Soft skills bring about a big change in the personality of the youngster. He begins to build good relationships, understands the value of a cheerful disposition. He knows how to handle stress and can manifest interpersonal skills in the work atmosphere. His interview skills improves a lot and his overall employability has a sea change.

What I am saying is that if young people especially those who lack confidence spend a little time on developing these skills, then their lives and careers will change.

I am sure my sharing these thoughts in this youngster friendly booklet will convey a passionate message I have for all youngsters out there.

"Success is not final, failure is not fatal: it is the courage to continue that counts."

— <u>*Winston Churchill*</u>

FOREWORD

Amidst the vast volumes of literature written on soft skills and their relevance in achieving success in life, this book from Dr. Rabindra Athri stands out distinctly. The learned author, with his profound knowledge and extensive experience in research and training in the specialized field of human resources and skill- development has brought out an excellent compendium on the concepts, methods and processes of harnessing and utilizing such select skills to unleash the power of a person within. This book comprehensively covers in good analytical detail, every aspect of the social, psychological, emotional, intellectual and behavioral traits of humans, as manifested in the finer qualities of the head and heart, which could be systematically moulded and groomed so as to instill the much needed self-esteem, self-realization and self-confidence in them. Dr. Athri has fully analyzed and comprehensively presented how these skills could be nurtured, nourished and applied through appropriate means, such as positive conversation, effective communication, binding social relationship, successful team building and excellent leadership.

While Dr. Athri has perceived the utility of this book essentially to bring about a dynamic change in the personality and competence of our youngsters that could propel them to heights of deserving success in their life and career, given its breadth, width and depth of content and coverage of practically the whole aspects of soft skills that shape the intrinsic internal as well as external images of a person, this book will equally be of immense help to aspiring professionals, business executives and managerial personnel of all ages to improve their vision, attitude, approach and application in dealing with complex situations that emerge at all times in day to day life.

This book will rank high as an authoritative text and manual, for those with innate latent potential within to succeed, but are unable to put their best foot forward and express and impress at the opportune time in the right manner. More importantly, this will be a valuable source of much needed practical knowledge and guidance to all who are ambitious, willing to learn and progress, whether they be professionals, practicing managers or entrepreneurs, enabling them to face problems, perform, excel and succeed.

Toward this, the "Soft Skill Initiative" as designed and concised by Dr. Athri, has clear and distinct objectives and dimensions. Firstly, it deals with the philosophy and phenomenon of human qualities of Self awareness, Positive Attitude, Self esteem, Motivation, Stress and Anger Management etc, the fine-tuning of which could make a person, balanced and matured enough. The book also deals extensively with the methods and processes of cultivating and developing these skill - sets to a level of enhancing the value and worth of the individual measured as his capacity to act fair in all situations, as it brings out objectively the benefits of the use of effective tools of formal and informal communication, Inter personal skills, negotiation skills, presentation skills etc. It further goes to demonstrate impressively how one has to move into the field of action, with visualization, goal setting, action plan and decision-making by providing the right leadership, ensuring managerial efficiency and achieving success in all deeds.

The intrinsic value of this book lies in that even a novice with not much knowledge or exposure of the nuances of the intricacies of soft skills could easily comprehend, learn systematically and develop confidently, the right attitude and the desired competence and capability needed to face trying situations with a positive frame of mind, understand their true genesis and significance in the right perspective, move ahead with finer values of empathy, sympathy and ethics, exercise assertiveness as needed and deliver as leader.

The learned author has convincingly explained all the concepts and processes of human faculties that collectively constitute the Soft Skills in simple language, with lucid instructions and guidance on how one has to carry out the tasks involved in the application of each of the skills steadily and step by step, by providing valid practical tips so that one could succeed, even amidst adversity.

This book is not to be read once and left on the shelf. It is a practice manual which has to be constantly and continuously referred to in the learning exercise, interpreted and applied to mould one's attitude and action at all levels and tested as to its effect and impact on success. It imparts powerful and practical lessons to be imbibed in intuitive ways.

I commend this book with full confidence that it would prove to be of valuable use and benefit to the young and old alike. It would help to discover and develop one's inherent potential fully, by getting over the 'dark spots' that lie deep in all of us and assist us to build on our emotional and intelligence quotient to de-mystify the complex problems that confront us in life and career, with cheer, and succeed in this challenging world of Conflict and Competition.

Venugopal C Govind
Varma&Varma,
Chartered Accountants,
Sriniketan, NettepadamRoad,
P.B. No.2350, Kochi-682016,
KeralaState(India)
Tel:(++91+484-2376323)
Fax:(++91+484-2376046)
E-mail: kochi@varmaandvarma.com
Website: www.varmaandvarma.com
****

The Power of confidence ....

OUR INDIA

India is a peaceful country.

We have never ever tried to acquire another country.

India's ability to survive challenges is phenomenal.

Today India is the fastest growing Economy.

Aditi Devo Bhava. We treat a guest as God.

Success for India is not wealth. It is spirituality and health.

We have the worlds greatest Epics.

We are taught that everyone is an Atma, so everyone is a brother or sister.

Respecting women is in our culture and tradition.

Belief and Hope are our key words.

We believe knowledge is the greatest wealth.

Nobody can steal it rob it

The Bhakthi and surrender culture is the core of India.

Freedom and tolerance are our values.

We need more Karmayogis.

Indias dharma emphasised Self restraint, nonviolance and compassion.

Einstein thought of Ahimsa as the single Indian word reflecting India.

Vasudeva Kutumbaha is the way India looks at the world. Today 50% of India is young. It is bound to be the No1 country in a few years

We are proud of our INDIA. **Dr. Rabindranath Athri**

9995449763

The Power of optimism ....]

Nothing Worth while is ever achieved
without deep thought and hard work.
One must think for oneself and never
accept anything at its face value, use slogans
and catch phrases to which, unfortunately,
our people are too easily susceptible.
One must for ever strive for excellence
or even perfection in any task however
small, and never be satisfied with the
second best.
Mob 9995449763

The Power of positive perception ......

.

The power of positive conversation ....

LIST OF SOFT SKILLS

Expression, The Positive Hello.
Self Awareness, Positive Perception, Positive Attitude, Positive Conversation.
Goal Setting, Action Plans.
Communication Skills, Nuances Of Communication Skills.
Formal And Informal Communication.
Distortions Of Communication.
Communication And Knowledge.
Communication And Feedback, Active Listening.
Business Communication.
Interpersonal Skills.
Relationships, Relationship And Learning.
Self Esteem.
Ownership, Empathy/Sympathy.
Leadership, Leader/Manager.
TeamDynamicsTeamBuilding.
Skill, Attitude, Success, Definitions Of Success.
Success Formulae, Consistency/Achievement.
How To Live In The Present. Practice Of Visualization.
Entrepreneurship, I Don't Take A NO.

Managerial Efficiency, I Am Born To Be A Star.
Motivation, Obstacles The Famous Teachers.
Persuasive Skills, Problem Solving.
Negotiation Skills, Conflict Management.
Stress Management, Assertive Skills.
Decision Making, Anger Management.
Presentation Skills, Ethics And Etiquettes.

"The true measure of success is how many times you can bounce back from failure."

— ***Stephen Richards***

EXPRESSION,
THE POSITIVE HELLO

In any kind of communication it is almost mandatory that the communicator should try and understand the mood of the listener at that point of time and also present an acceptable and friendly expression to the listener. We say that this is mandatory because a communicator with a specific objective has to get an idea even if it is partial of the mindset of the listener. The listener has to basically perceive the facial expression and the manifestations of the body language of the communicator. This first impression can make all the difference and decide the success or otherwise of achieving the objective of the communicator.

Here the term Expression is like saying a 'Positive Hello'. Normally how careful are we when we meet a person for the first time or even for the nth time? Whatever the case maybe, when a person is approaching someone else for a particular purpose, if his facial expressions are genuine, he has a cheerful and energetic disposition and also a positive smile, it is more likely to be perceived by the other person as a happy encounter resulting in the latter being interested in interacting with the communicator.

It goes without saying that if the expression is neithercheerful, nor positive, nor attractive, then the communicator himself and his proposal is likely to be poor, and consequently the whole interaction by the communicator goes flat. For some experts however, it is possible to overcome this initial draw back throughthe use of excellent content, presentation and closing.

It is said that the first impression (with a good expression) is the best impression.

The good expressions and impressions that we make often result in the success of our communication with others.

Mother Teresa – "Peace begins with a smile."

"I want freedom for the full expression of my personality."
     — Mahatma Gandhi, The Essential Gandhi:
          An Anthology of His Writings on His Life, Work, and Ideas

SELF AWARENESS

Everyhuman failure, whether it be sorrow or depression, frustration or suspicion, anything that causes suffering to the body mind or soul is basically due to lack of self-awareness. Achieving self awareness helps one to attain a balanced state of existence. However this is not some sort ofrocket science.

Self Awareness and Relationships

We humans are social beings. Therefore, relationships are very important for us. Since one is never a loner, one has to develop the skill of relationship building. For this reason one has to know oneself thoroughly, i.e., one's own strengths, weaknesses, attitudes and moods. Only then can one interact sensibly with others around him.

This is true, whether it is at your workplace or in your personal life. When you can change the way you interpret what's on your mind, for instance your thoughts, then you can change your emotions as well and there will be a shift in the emotional quality of your relationships. When you make this shift happen in you, it opens up entirely new possibilities in your life.

Having a clear understanding of your thought and, behavior patterns helps you understand other people. This ability to empathize facilitates better personal and professional relationships.

Develop Self Awareness

Self awareness is developed when you begin to practice in focusing your attention on the details of your personality and behavior. It isn't learned from reading a book. When you read a book you are focusing your attention on the conceptual ideas in the book.

While reading a book, you are not paying attention to your own behavior, emotions and personality.

"Everything that irritates us about others can lead us to an understanding of ourselves."

— *C.G. Jung*

Developing one's self awareness is like learning how to dance. When one learns to dance, one has to pay attention to the movements of one's feet, hands and body and also what the other partner or dancers are doing. One should also be aware of the music, the beats and the floor space.

Learning is a multiplex process. In this process you read, you understand, you think, you accept, you decide to take it into your life and possibly implement the concept that you like. This process is also a step towards obtaining self awareness. What you learn is important for you and if you want to practice it, one good way is to share what you have learnt with somebody, discuss it with somebody and you can keep this concept in your conversations with anybody.

BUILDING A POSITIVE PERCEPTION

Everything in life can be compared to a two sided coin. One can see just one side of the coin and decide to be happy and spread happiness to others around. This in general is considered as a positive perception.

On the other hand if one chooses the other side of the coin one is going to see many reasons to be sorrowful, angry, frustrated, jealous etc.

However one has a choice over this matter and cannot blame anybody else for choosing any one side of the coin.

There are many situations in life where one's perception can either be positive or negative. Some examples are:

You get busier at work and, consequently, you have to work harder and longer. A positive perception would be that there is an increasing demand for your work which means there is a greater likelihood that you and your company will be more successful and achieve your financial and career objectives. People with a negative point of view would complain they have less free time.

"We are all in the gutter, but some of us are looking at the stars."
— *Oscar Wilde, Lady Windermere's Fan*

My next post will talk about purity in thought and in deeds.

POSITIVE ATTITUDE

These two words are extremely powerful, highly meaningful and very relevant in today's circumstances.

What do we understand by POSITIVE. This is often depending on the context.

It is the choice we take between two options in front of us.

The general meaning of POSITIVE is a perception by choice to start with, which evolves into something good, harmonious, peaceful and relaxing to oneself and others around us. This perception is also healthy for the perceiver. This is a habit we make once we realize the futility and even danger of negative perception.

Perception is the first step to positive attitude.

Attitude is simply what we are, our traits, our behavior and our type so to say. How we respond or react to something is a sign of our attitude.

Attitude evolves from childhood, to external circumstances which decides our beliefs, likes and dislikes, our approach and our style of conversation.

Attitude is a good part of the image we build in the minds of people around us.

Small changes can make a huge difference in our personality.

A positive attitude is a winner attitude. Seeing the best part of things, events, conversations and life as a whole. A switch on is easy and quick. It can also be tough and impossible to others.

GOAL SETTING

In life, goal setting is the most critical single act one has to do inorder to succeed "by success in life I do not mean just economical or money oriented success. Success can be measured in many values which you think is your goal among the six areas which are congruent to the term "success". You can decide how much importance you give to success in the following six areas, Family and Home, Financial and Career, Spiritual and Ethical, Physical and Health, Social and Cultural, Mental and Educational. A good mix of these factors can help you set a goal for yourself.

Goals can be personal and familial, like going for a flat, a car or a jewel set, which are important goals for the family growth.

Goals can be professional like aiming for a promotion, increment, change of job etc. which are obvious steps towards professional growth.

Social goals can be where one tries to join elite clubs, like Rotary, Lions, Yacht clubs or maybe going for a luxury car etc. to step up in the social ladder.

Physical and heath goals can be to trim down weight, take up yoga, join the gym, etc. with the objective of trimming your weight and ensure good health.

> *"Aim higher in case you fall short."*
> — *Suzanne Collins, Catching Fire*

Educational goal can be something like joining for a research program, getting a PhD and becoming a professor, this can also be a social goal.

When someone asks himself some typical spiritual questions like "who am I", "where have I come from", "what is the purpose of my existence", then he is on the path to a spiritual goal, because he wants to know the answers to these questions. Write your goal in the positive instead of the negative. By all means, make sure your goal is high enough. Write down your goals.

Goals with time frames

A goal without a time frame actually is not a goal. Small goals correctly timed will ensure that the big goal will come in time.

Prioritize your goals.

Create a step-by-step plan.

All goals have to be focused to growth.

Goals are decided on the basis of what we want to achieve along with our strengths and weaknesses.

Goal setting is not only for life it is also for every productive and professional activity.

"It is good to have an end to journey toward; but it is the journey that matters, in the end."

— <u>*Ernest Hemingway*</u>

Check the gap between knowledge and actual doing ....

COMMUNICATION SKILLS

Communication skills are called the mother of all skills. Whether it is relationship building which is critical to a human being or getting things done on time which are the skills necessary for a manager or just conveying some information to another person or public speaking which is a big confidence builder, one should be aware that proper communication skills are required if one's efforts and success are to go hand in hand. Negotiation skills, selling skills, counseling skills, all these come under the umbrella of communication skills.

Verbal communication is restricted to what words and languages are used for during interactions and nonverbal are a plethora of skills which highlight and boost the efficiency of the verbal language.

Experts of communication and behavioral sciences confirm that verbal communication has an effect of just 7 % on the listener.

The rest 93% is dominated by body language, eye contact, voice modulation, the hmms and oos which are only sounds but convey meaning according to the specific situation. Silence is another powerful tool of communication.

Body Language

Body language is the various movements we manifest to enhance the effect of the communication. Through gestures with hands, head, shoulders and posture of the body etc., we show emphasis, doubt, assurance and confidence and this tool of body language makes all the difference between a powerful, effective speech and a dull one.

"The single biggest problem with communication is the illusion that it has takenplace."

— *George Bernard Shaw*

We can learn how to use this tool by taking part in training programs, observing good speech makers in the T.V. or attending speeches given by powerful speakers.

Eye contact

Eye contact is a critical tool in communication. It is a very powerful tool to convey very subtle messages which in some situations cannot be conveyed by words for example, in an interview situation we cannot tell the interviewer that we are trustworthy, honest, sincere etc. these messages can be conveyed only by the effective use of eye contact and nuances of eye messaging.

Voice modulation

Voice modulation has an important role in communication. The basic point is that you can' convey different meanings by the way you modulate your voice.

Everybody understands that the difference in meaning in different voice modulations. Howevera study and practice of the numerousmodulations will help one to master the art of good and effective communication.

The 'hmms' and 'oos'

This is another category of communication without words. Here the communicator either by habits or by intentions avoid any verbal communication and choose only sounds like 'hmms', 'oos' and 'aah', to convey his response. This tool is also understood by most of the listeners. So it is prudent to use this tool which will convey the message and possibly minimize the reaction.

Silence

Strictly speaking silence is a very powerful tool which can convey more than words. That is why it is said in the guru shishia relationships in the days of yore that the guru would remain silent most of the time while the shishia would ask the questions.

"Self-consciousness kills communication."

— Rick Steves

The guru's silence conveyed to the shishia that the former wants the latter to think and go deeper. Some times the guru would nod his encouragement or approve the direction in which the shishia was going.

In day to day life where there are conflicts, which are sometimes irrational like in homes, silence can be an excellent healer. It is said you need two hands to clap; ifone hand chooses not to clap, then how can there be noise ? This is an excellent solution for those frequent and irrational quarrels that occur in our homes.

Nuance of Communication Skill

The intricacy of the most important aspect of everyone's life is proper communication skills, whether the communication takes place at the commerce and business level or at the social level. The word 'communication' as such is derived from the Latin word 'communis' which means common; that is, the sender and receiver of the message must understand the same thing in the same sense.

Features of communication

When closely analysed, the features of communication have two parts, a sender and a receiver of the message. Transfer of information is a continuous process, which should permeate at all levels of management. A feedback for the information given is a component of the communication.

When examined why an effective communication is so important, a few facts become oblivious. Firstly an effective communication facilitates effective planning, secondly it helps in proper decision making, thirdly it improves the relation among the employees, fourthly it brings about co-ordination in the working atmosphere, and fifthly it becomes a great motivator for people in an organisation.

> *"Constantly talking isn't necessarily communicating."*
> — *Charlie Kaufman*

Types of communication

Communication is considered as the mother of all skills. Whether it is used to build a relationship or a skill to get things done or skills that are meant to be passed down or negotiating skills or counseling skills etc every skill comes from the platform of communication skills.

Basically there are four types of communication skills

1. Advice oriented communication.
2. Criticism oriented communication.
3. Content oriented communication.
4. Feeling oriented communication.

Advice oriented communication refers to the commonly encountered unwarranted advice that most parents and seniors keep giving to disinterested audience. This is even more irritating because it is repeated very often.

The only exception where an advice is taken well is when someone elseasks for advice and then the advice is given. Here the advice is sought, so it is welcome.

Criticism oriented communication. Very often we see somebody who criticizes just to criticize. Your top does not match with your jeans, your hair - do is not ok for you. Such negative criticisms are seen very often in one's day - to - daylife. This type of criticism is irritating and sometimes even disgusting. However if somebody asks for your suggestion about something he/she did and you give some positive suggestions for the purpose of improving, then it is welcome. In other words if criticism is asked for, it is liked and welcomed. But if it is given when it is not asked for, then it is totally disliked.

"You have to lift a person up before you can really put them in their place."
— *Criss Jami*

Content oriented communication is when emphasis is given to the contents or facts conveyed through the communication. Here the communicator is not trying to advice or criticize, but is just conveying the actual matter and normally there is very good acceptance for a content oriented communication. For example, when a speaker says, "thirty percent of India's population remains hungry" or "India's future is safe in the hands of our youngsters who consist of 50% of our population", then the audience is more likely to fully accept this message given by the speaker.

Communication experts suggest that the first way of starting a conversation or a speech is to start with a content oriented communication.

Feeling oriented communication is one that brings about emotional change in the listener. The typical example of this kind of communication would be a four year old child asking for ice-cream from the father. The child tactically brings about a change in the mind of the father by saying,"daddy you promised me ice-cream for getting the first prize in recitation, you must get me ice-cream now".

A person seeking donation says, "In Cochin we have 20,000 destitute children and we are now looking after nearly 7000 by providing food shelter and education. Your donation will help us to support a few more children." Here the seeker of donation has created a feeling in the mind of the listener and so he is likely to get a donation.

If one understands these 4 basic types of communication, the mind will open up to thousands of types of communication.

> *"Write to be understood, speak to be heard, read to grow."*
> — *Lawrence Clark Powell*

Discover the magic of communication in conversations between a teacher and a student, between a doctor and thepatient, between a mother and her daughter, between a father and his son, between a banker and a customer, between a customer and a textile sales person and thousands like this. If we think and focus on the myriads of such communication then possibly you will come to a stage where you will apply the right style, the right mode, the right toll etc and that will be your journey to mastery of communication skills.

A communication in an organization could be downward where the message travels from the boss to all the lower levels or upward from the lower level to the boss or side wards to different personnel at the same level. Again communication could be formal like a business notification or informal like loose schedules for a forthcoming time frame. Yet again the communication could be verbal or written or non verbal or gestural.

Communication process

How does the process of communication take place? Thebasic and simple process of communication takes place when a message or an idea or a thought developed needs to be communicated. It could be an opinion or a feeling or a view which needs to be transferred. The next step is the encoding message that includes transferring a gesture or words or visuals. Then comes channelizing the message that is to plan how many would receive this message, nature of the message, cost and time required, and to organize the feedback for the message transmitted. Next, the message is decoded. This involves the receiver interpretingthe message into meaningful information which may require a response.

"it's important to make sure that we're talking with each other in a way that heals, not in a way that wounds." - Barack Obama, 44 th U.S. President.

In the process of communication the major setback visualised is the "Noise" in other words, the factors that disturbs, confuses, and interferes with effective communication. This noise could be external or internal.

Finally the feedback or the reaction to the communication expressed. If the feedback is positive then the communication process is effective and there is a minimised noise level in the channel through which the message is communicated.

Communication Barriers

There are four major barriers for any effective communication. They are language barriers, psychological barriers, physical barriers and other barriers.

A language barrier often occurs while communicating. It could be poorly chosen words or limitation in the range of language used or poor translation or poorly constructed sentences which distort the meaning.

A psychological barrier occurs when human emotions like attitude, feelings, perception, values etc interfere in the processing of communication by the receiver.

Physical barriers occurs when the communication gets distorted by noise, extreme heat or cold, poor ventilation or any other physical discomforts like hunger, thirst, stress etc.

Other barriers includes inconsistency between verbal and nonverbal communication like distrust, presumptions, non-precise communication etc.

"The most important thing in communication is to hear what isn't being said."

— Peter Drucker

Effective Communication

The golden rule of effective communication could be summarized as follows:

Clarity in thought in conveying message, purpose behind the communication, catering to the sensitive needs of the receiver, usage of appropriate language, credibility in the communication and delivering at appropriate settings, some of the essential requirement.

Finally the communicator should have good voice control and good expression and above all should be a good listener for any feedback that may be generated.

Formal and Informal Communication

Communication can be formal and informal. However, formal communication does not mean written communication. For example, a verbal reprimand from a manager to a subordinate is a form of formal communication, whereas a written joke passed around the office is a form of informal communication. The purposes of informal communication are (1) to satisfy personal needs; (2) to prevent boredom; (3) to provide information relevant to the job that is not provided by formal channels.

Some Reasons for Communication Distortions

When we listen to others, we tend to evaluate them on the basis of their statements and hence we interpret what is being said thereafter according to our first impressions. For example, if a person makes a few initial unfavorable remarks about religion, we tend to brand him as an agnostic and will view the rest of the message in that light.

"We are stronger when we listen, and smarter when we share."
— ___Rania Al-Abdullah___

Advanced Information

Advanced information can cause us to favor certain interpretations and reject other informations. When we receive information that we believe to be accurate, we may tend to structure subsequent information in a way that is consistent with our prior knowledge.

Lack of Interest

This reason will cause communication distortions even many messages may be received because the message was never interpreted consciously by the receiver.

Distrust

If someone distrusts the sender, he or she is likely to distort or change the message negatively to accommodate his or her personal feelings.

Ways to Reducing Communication Distortions

Encourage Feedback

Sender must make sure they receive feedback cues from receivers in order to know how well they can be transmitting the accuracy of message.

Developing Trust

Information should be perceived to be informative, rather than manipulative in order to develop trust and prevent distortion.

Repetition

If we think something is particularly important, it might be worth while to say the same thing in two or three ways even if it proves redundant.

> *"Art is communication."*
> — *Madeleine L'Engle*, *Walking on Water:*
> *Reflections on Faith and Art*

Listening with Understanding

It means to see from the other person's point of view. For example, a third party, who is able to lay aside his own feelings and evaluations, can assist greatly by listening with understanding to each person and clarifying the views and issues.

Use the problem- solving approach

The problem solving approach is effective in that it creates an atmosphere of trust and openness, by inviting subordinates to contribute ideas engaging in two way communication.

"When the trust account is high, communication is easy, instant, and effective."
— **Stephen R. Covey, *The 7 Habits of Highly Effective People: Powerful Lessons in Personal Change***

Communication Feedback

Active Listening - Listening skills fuel our social, emotional and professional success, and studies prove that listening is a skill we can learn.

The Technique. Active listening is really an extension of the Golden Rule. To know how to listen to someone else, think about how you would want to be listened to.

While the ideas are largely intuitive, it might take some practice to develop (or re-develop) the skills. Here's what good listeners know — and you should, too:

"We have two ears and one mouth, so we should listen more than we say."
— **Zeno of Citium, as quoted by Diogenes Laërtius**

What are Interpersonal Skills?

Interpersonal skills are the life skills we use every day to communicate and interact with other people, individually and in groups.

Interpersonal skills include not only how we communicate with others, but also our confidence, and our ability to listen and understand. Problem solving, decision making and personal stress managements are also considered interpersonal skills.

People with strong interpersonal skills are usually more successful in both their professional and personal lives. They are perceived as more calm, confident and charismatic, qualities that are often endearing or appealing to others. Being more aware of your interpersonal skills can help you improve and develop them. We provide an extensive library of articles to help you learn about and improve your interpersonal skills.

"If conversation was the lyrics, laughter was the music, making time spent together a melody that could be replayed over and over without getting stale."

— <u>*Nicholas Sparks*</u>

Reflect and Improve

Think about previous conversations and other interpersonal interactions; learn from your mistakes and successes. Always keep a positive attitude but realize that we can all always improve our <u>communicative skills</u>.

Interpersonal skills

Smile.
Manifest appropriate body language.
Be appreciative.
Pay attention to others.

Practice active listening.

Bring people together.

Recognize and resolve conflicts well in time.

Communicate clearly.

Humor them.

Empathize.

Don't complain.

Bust interpersonal stress as soon as you notice it.

A kinesthetic touch helps in building relationships.

Have a transparency in your attitude.

Praise more, criticize less.

"If you have nothing to say, say nothing."
— Mark Twain

The power of empathy in interpersonal relation ....

RELATIONSHIPS, RELATIONSHIP AND LEARNING

Research has found that while trying to learn something, such as a new technique or skill, there is a four stage process at work. This learning process extends to improving your relationship skills as well. You just don't go from a total novice to an expert right away. It is a gradual process where you first start to learn about and realize the things you have been doing wrong and bring your attention to them before you can start to correct them.

Self Esteem

Self esteem is your opinion of yourself. High self esteem is a good opinion of yourself and low self esteem is a bad opinion of yourself.

"When one realises one is asleep, at that moment one is already half-awake."

— *P.D. Ouspensky*

"A company is only as good as its people."-Jack Stack.

Empathy vs. Sympathy

Empathy and **Sympathy** are relationships based on shared <u>emotions</u> and understanding. Empathy is understood as the ability to mutually experience the thoughts, emotions, and direct experience of others without them being directly communicated intentionally.

Sympathy is a feeling of care and understanding for suffering beings.

Both have similar usage but differ in their emotional meaning.

Comparison chart

	Empathy	Sympathy
Example:	I can empathise with how aggrieved you must be at the loss of your beloved.	I offer my sympathy at the loss of your loved one.
Relationship:	Friends, Family, Community	Poor and less fortunate: may include disadvantaged members of friends, family and community

	Empathy	**Sympathy**
Definition:	The ability to co-experience and relate to the thoughts, emotions, or experience of others without them being communicated directly by the individual	The ability to understand and to support the emotional situation or experience of another being with compassion and sensitivity
Feeling:	An empath can consciously or unconsciously take on the illness, afflictions or emotions of another.	One can sympathize without "taking on" (or experiencing) what the other is going through or feeling.
Scope:	Personal	From either one to another person or one to many (or one to a group or issue)
Easy Definition:	Identifying with or experiencing vicariously another's thoughts, feelings, or attitudes. To feel their pain.	Feel sorry for; Feel pity for; Feel bad for.
Emotion:	Close bonded relationships.	Care, Protection.
Relative to:	Caring, Personal Growth.	Wisdom, Charity.

Obstacles are the famous teachers

"History has demonstrated that the most notable winners usually encountered heartbreaking obstacles before they triumphed. They won because they refused to become discouraged by their defeats."

The art of persuasion teaches one how to get others to see things his or her way.

PROBLEM SOLVING

The whole problem with Problem Solving is almost always the feeling that problem is a big problem and this difficult answer is unlikely to be solved.

This feeling enhances the so called problem due to the building up of tension, stress and sometimes panic.

Experienced individuals know and say that every problem has a solution.

Every problem in this timeframe of universal time has been solved, some quickly, and some over a period of time.

Man certainly is an emotional person, but it all depends on where you put the emotion. If it's on the Problem, the solution will take time, ideas to solve will possibly not strike.

So the first thing to do is Face the problem squarely.

Believe it has a solution.

Step by step understand what exactly is the problem. Very often this step will bring out a solution.

Break the problem into small bits as per sequence.

Think and work out steps to take to solve the small problems, looking at options at every stage.

Stabilise on the workable options.

At every stage do not forget to take the guidance of people around who are experienced. Often that will ease the way out.

Take the approach of a positive sportsperson.

Be careful about taking risks. But do not be afraid of taking a risk if your homework is pakka.

Creativity, or thinking or doing differently is key to problem solving.

"If I had an hour to solve a problem I'd spend 55 minutes thinking about the problem and 5 minutes thinking about solutions."
— Albert Einstein

Do you realize that you have many interviews in life …. Be prepared

WHY PRE- INTERVIEW PREPARATION?

- TO KNOW ABOUT THE COMPANY.
- TO KNOW THE WORKING CONDITION.
- TO KNOW MY JOB PROFILE.
- TO CONFIRM THE PROPER DRESS CODE.

WHAT DO I DO DURING THE INTERVIEW.

- BE READY WITH TECHNICAL SUBJECT KNOWLEDGE.
- GOOD COMMAND OF ENGLISH.

- LIST OUT ALL POSSIBLE QUESTION THAT HE MAY ASK, STARTING FROM SELF INTRODUCTION.
- WE SHOULD SHOW GOOD EXPRESSION.
- PROPER EYE CONTACT THAT SHOWS THAT WE ARE TRUSTWORTHY.
- CONFIDENCE IN THE PERSON.
- THE RIGHT PERSON.
- WE SHOULD SHOW CORRECT BODY LANGUAGE THAT IS
- CORRECT BODY POSTURE.
- CORRECT GESTURE.
- IF THERE ARE MORE THAN ONE PERSONS WE SHOULD GIVE ATTENTION TO ALL.

INTERVIEW FOLLOW UP?

- MAKE A FOLLOW UP PHONE CALL A FEW DAYS AFTER THE INTERVIEW. IT WILL SHOW YOUR KEEN INTEREST TO JOIN THAT COMPANY.
- TRY TO CONTACT THE HR DEPARTMENT STAFF, THROUGH E-MAIL.

*Practice the step and sequent of you answers to possible questions ....
You will get five offer letters and you can choose one ...... I said you
are the boss*

Self Introduction-TELL ME ABOUT YOURSELF

My name is xxxx xxxx. My home town is xxxx xxx. I am from a loving average middle class family. My father xxx xx is a business man. My mother xxx xxx is a home maker. I have two sisters who are both married. I done my 10th and got distinction at xxxxxxxxx, my +2 at xxx and got a first class and did my btech at xxxxxx and got first class in that as well. During my school and college days I had participated in recitation, singing, and dance competitions. I got 1st prize in puppet making, 2 times in district level during my school days.

How were your school days?

It was the best part of my life. It was full of joy. I have a great company of friends. Our teachers were committed. It was an interesting stage of learning. *What about your extracurricular activities?*

In my school days I participated in poem recitation, singing competition. In 8th and 9th I got first prize 2 times in district level for puppet making. That was my favourite hobby because it involves a lot of planning, creativity and visualizing. I made a crocodile puppet which I can operate with my own fingers. In college days I have participated in group dance.

Have you organized anything on your own?

During my college days I organized a team for group dance. I was their inspiration for making our group. I trained them and made an entertaining presentation.

How do you convey that you are an honest trust worthy, sincere person ……. Only by good eye contact techniques…….

Who is your favourite teacher and why?

My favourite teacher is Antony Anburaj. He is the one who has the skill to teach and make students understand. He is very friendly to all, but he knows when to be strict also.

Tell us about your friends?

I have lots of friends from school to work. During my work in gulf I used to keep in touch with many of my friends through the internet. Nowadays other than these friends I keep in touch with my school friendswho are here.

What is your weakness?

Sir, sometimes I find it difficult to understand people. I am trying to get over it by empathetic understanding and by focusing on what I want to understand. By this I am able to understand them better. I watch my mind carefully and take rational decisions.

Why you think that you should be taken here?

Sir, I am a fast learner. I am very friendly with my colleagues and I try to keep very healthy relation with them. I worked with seniors who were all friendly with me and ready to guide me. I am thorough in the fundamentals with my subject and have some valuable experience.

Do people generally like you, why?

I am a friendly person. I maintain relationships in a good manner. I have a good sense of humor and I am open minded and flexible.

Remember and high light your strengths and clearly convey how the company will benefit by taking you ...... if you do this you have got it..........

A LIST OF OTHER POSSIBLE QUESTIONS FOR WHICH YOU CAN PREPARE SUITABLE ANSWERS REFLECTING A LEARNING ATITTUDE AND OPEN MIND

SCHOOL

1. What are the subjects you liked in school?
2. Which subject did you score maximum marks in? Why?
3. Please describe your favourite teacher in school?
4. Please describe your best friend at school?
5. What are the games that you played most at school?
6. Please describe your school?
7. Please tell us about your favourite hobby during school going age?
8. Tell about your school annual day. How did you participate?
9. Which movie did you like the most during your school days? Why?
10. Describe your most memorable experience at school?

11. What did you learnt from school?
12. Would you admit your (future) children to the same school?
13. Which teacher were you scared of in school? why?
14. How many teachers are you in touch with ? why?
15. Tell us something about your farewell at your school?
16. What was the most embarrassing moment during your school days?
17. Which was the occasion you are most proud off in school days?
18. What kind of competition did you have in your school?
19. What activities did you have on your sports days?
20. Have you ever hidden your progress report from your parents? How, and what did you do?
21. Have you helped your parents in any way during your school days? How?
22. What social activities did you participate when in school?
23. Were you ever part of scouts/guides or NCC? What made you participate?
24. What was your reaction when your neighbor had a tv and you did not?
25. What would you and your friends do when you had a free hour in school?

An interview is a challenge if you don't prepare and practice...... if you prepare and practice an interview is just a friendly conversation for the HR Man to know you ....

EXTRACURRICULAR ACTIVITIES

1. What are your hobbies?
2. Tell me more about your favourite hobby.
3. Which news paper(s) do you read regularly? Why do you prefer this news paper?
4. What pages in the news paper interest you the most? How much time do you spend on these pages every day?
5. What magazines do you read regularly? Why do you prefer these magazines?
6. What are the programs that you watch on TV? How much time do you spend watching them daily?
7. Which program on TV do you like most? Why? Who makes this program? Tell more about this program?
8. Who is your favourite tv star /starlet? Why?
9. What are your views on tv as a medium of communication?
10. Which is your favourite movie? Tell us more on this movie. Why has is made an impact on you?
11. How does you hobby help you?
12. How often do you browse the internet? How much time do you spend every week on the net?
13. Why do you use the internet? How has it help you?
14. What are your interests outside the college? Tell us more about them.
15. What is the most memorable experience that you have in your area of interest? Tell us about it.
16. It is believed that old film music is better. What do you have to say?

17. Do you believe that tv is stopping people reading? Why?
18. Do you believe that tv is stopping people from socializing? Why?
19. How did you explain, when you were caught stealing fruits from other's garden?
20. Do you know how to ride a cycle describe you first ride.
21. Tell us about the first cricket match you played.
22. Do you remember the first painting you made? What was it?
23. Describe the first important match that you won.
24. What kind of music do you like? Why? Name three of your favourite musicians?
25. Do you wish that you learnt to change that fused bulb at home? Why?

Please do not hide your weakness .... He will find out..... Convey how your presently doing your best to overcome the weakness

LIIKES/DISLIKES/ASPIRATIONS/TASTES

1. Whom do you respect the most amongst your friends? Why?
2. Who do you respect the most in your family? Why?
3. What would you describe as your most important moment of achievement? Tell us about it.
4. How would your closes friend describe you?
5. Who is the political leader you respect most? Why?
6. Who is the sports person you admire most? Why?

7. What task do you prefer doing most? Tell us ore about it.
8. Which advertisement on the tv do you like most? Why?
9. What would you like to be five years later?
10. What is the action for which you have been most appreciated by your parents? Please describe.
11. What are the learning's you have imbibed fro your parents? Describe.
12. How do you want your parents look at you?
13. How would you be able to contribute to society after completion of the MBA?
14. What do you want your colleagues to talk about you?
15. Who in your view, amongst those you know, is the most successful? Why?
16. Who in your view, amongst those you know, is the happiest? Why?
17. Who is your role model? Why?
18. Describe your ideal first job.
19. How will you want your friends to think of you?
20. For what do you want to be remembered.
21. You hate going on the giant wheel, but your friends are forcing you to. How will you manage?

The more interview you attend the more experienced and confident you become ...... attend every possible interview ...... you will see improvement

EMOTIONS

1. What makes you happy?
2. Describe situations that make you angry?
3. What qualities do you dislike in people?
4. Were you ever made "April fool", what was your reaction?
5. Have you ever stayed away from your parents? How did you miss them?
6. If you were to become a cartoon character, who will you become?
7. Do you share your success and failures with your parents? If not with whom?
8. You worked hard to submit an assignment, which your teacher dislikes, what will you do?
9. Were you faced with a situation to lend a shoulder to support your friend on a difficult situation? What did you do?
10. What will be our reaction if we reject your mba applications?
11. Have you ever felt cheated? Why?
12. If you were to win a lottery of 1 crore what will you do?
13. How will you react if everything seems to be going wrong on a particular day?
14. How did you feel when your parents refused to sent you on a picnic for which all of your friends were going?
15. What was your state of mind while standing in a ticket counter I the railways?

16. Your friend breaks your favourite pen. how will you react?

17. You find the first greeting card you received in life, stolen. How will you dead with it?

18. Your pet dog is found missing when you go back home from college. How will you react?

19. Which poem inspires you most? Why?

20. Which story which was told to you when you were a child, do you still remember? What is the reason?

21. What did you do when your parents refused to buy you that video game which everyone in town had?

22. What do you do now, when your parents deny permission for you to go for evening movie with friends?

23. What memories do you have of your earliest birthday celebrations?

24. Do you find that people around you are worse than you are, but are teacher's pets? How do you deal with these situations?

25. You actually did a very difficult assignment, but your friend copied it and submitted it before you. How will you take it up with your friend?

Most questions are only to find your response and reaction..... take it easy and respond positively with smiling face ......

QUALITIES

1. Do people generally like you? Why?
2. How often do you watch movies? What do you do when you don't like the movie that the whole group is going to?
3. Why do you want to do an MBA?
4. Can you move to a new city and settle down quickly, how?
5. Have you conducted any activity in your school/ college? Did you have any issues with your friends? What? And how did you resolve them?
6. What are the qualities of a good manager? Of these which do you have?
7. How do you define success?
8. If you are to do well in a group assignment, how will you mange it?
9. What will you do when others come late for a drama/ music practice session?
10. If there is just one parachute left with you and a child in the crashing plane, what will you do?

Be prepared to answer "why do you say that"...... prepare and practice ......

DO YOU WANT TO BECOME A LEADER?

People often envision themselves as a leader for whatever reasons. But it takes some special qualities required to lead, telling you how to go about acquiring these qualities and constantly better them in order to remain at the top and a leader always.

Leaders are born not made. Would you agree with that statement? To some extent some natural leadership talent is of course an advantage; more important perhaps is the passion for the art of leadership and a desire to constantly improve through further skill development.

Many people take on leadership roles because they like the prestige, or see leadership as career progression and the only development path worth taking

Leadership doesn't have one single definition it is a combination of taking charge build a team, recognize the role of team members and take them along to the winners post.....

WHY BE A LEADER?

The first leadership tip is doing go into it for those reasons alone. Let's face it; there is so much diversity in today's career opportunities that if status and money arc your goals there are plenty of ways achieving these without having to lead teams of people. As the name implies leadership involves taking other people with you. It should never be viewed as a profession like accountancy, law or engineering and must be studied. When did you last read a book on leadership? If your answer was never or a year ago or so ago, it might be time to review your commitment to your profession.

CAN YOU BE VERSATILE?

You should enjoy the challenges of working with and generating productivity out of people. Can you accommodate lots of different personal styles? If you are going to lead anything more than one or more people this becomes unavoidable.

LEADERSHIP BEHAIOUR

Everything you do or say as a leader is amplified insignificance beyond all reasons. If you arrive in your department or business noticeably tense your staff will pick up on this in a micro seconds and assign all sorts of reason for this behavior. There are documented examples whose tension and impatient behavior have been interpreted as the impending closure of the business.

"Our chief want is someone who will inspire us to be what we know we could be."

— *Ralph Waldo Emerson*

LEADERSHIP

LEADERSHIP COMMUNICATION SKILLS

The leader never stops communication even when he or she isn't intending to. There frankly no point being balanced, measured and motivated when you think the focus is on you at meetings or "brining it on" like a second rate politician. You need to be consistent for people to buy into you. On and by the way consistently bad tempered is not an option. You are in the spot light all the time even off duty.

ALWAYS HAVE STRATEGIES

You should always have strategy! This is a key domain of leadership. If you don't know where the business is going then how can you expect everyone else to? Try to make strategy simple, relevant achievable and easy to understand. Above all it should be summarized into a few simple headline statement and then communicated again and again.....................And just when you think everyone has got it ....Think again!

CREATE POSITIVE ENVIRONMENT

Make yours a fun place to be in. a certain amount of stress can be useful. This kind of stress and pressure that comes about when a motivated team of people striving to get the job completed can be quite liberating. This kind of stress that comes about through exhaustion, insecurity, working in a disharmonious environment and frankly being too serious can be highly unproductive. Seek opportunity for some lightheartedness and fun and try to convey sense f certainty. People don't like bad news or worry.

A leader evolves or gets elected unanimously ….. he is not thrust on the team

LEADERSHIP AND DEVELOPMENT

Finally! Let your people blossom. This might sound very fluffy but it's one of the great leadership secrets and if you take one thing away from this page today let that be it. If you seek and take all the glory, then hopefully you are prepared all of the pressure and the blame when thins o wrong9as they certainly will at some point). Indeed, the proverbial buck might well stop with you but as another great saying reminds us…Leaders are about their worst team member. If this is correct you might want to think about developing the skill set of your staff and recognizing the contributions made by them.

FEELING OF OWNERSHIP

OWNERSHIP-THE BEST MOTIVATION

- ➢ The feeling that my work and work spot is mine.
- ➢ I feel this is my business. Yes somebody is paying me, this is not important here.
- ➢ I enjoy my work.
- ➢ My self image is related to my job performance.
- ➢ My job performance is very important to me.
- ➢ My responsibility is more than my contractual obligation.
- ➢ It is not my desire to stick to my organization. It's myself concept that matters.
- ➢ It's a feeling I cannot explain or describe.

Ownership comes from the heart and the result fantastic ....

HISTORY

The history of the 8 billionaires in the world shows that none of them had gone beyond 8th standard and all of them started at the bottom and worked their way up. Every one of them enjoyed the ownership feeling at every stage. They continue to enjoy this feeling and encourage their workers to feel like owners.

Great managers who have the ownership feeling had the guts to take risks. The board of directors of a Gold loan company in Kerala voted against the company to go pan India with over 2000 branches. The MD was confident in his heart, due to ownership feeling, and went ahead with his plan, and in 2 years the company has over 2000 branches and over 2400 cores turnover.

An extremely innovative shipping Engineer always passionately believed that Indian brains are the best in the world for maintenance, repair and reuse. He passionately talked about it and did some of the most innovative miracles in the shipping industry.

All that Mahatma Gandhi did for the country was because he thought and believed that he belongs to India and India belongs to him.

Swami Vivekananda breathed India, talked India and Lived India.

"Ownership breeds slavery: with every single thing that you acquire, comes a new worry of not losing that thing."
— *Mokokoma Mokhonoana*

BENEFITS OF GREATER OWNERSHIP

➢ I Take Pride In My Work And Its Success.
➢ Work Hard And Diligently.
➢ Work smarter and more productively.
➢ I walk the extra mile.
➢ Show a good example to others.

> ➤ More likely to get leadership.
> ➤ Greater job satisfaction.
> ➤ High degree of personal ownership to institution.
> ➤ Perception is more positive.
> ➤ Learn in the process.

HOW DO I GET MY COLLEAUES TO GET OWNERSHIP FEELING

> ➤ Help; show them how to work smarter.
> ➤ Take the bull by the horn...not quit.
> ➤ Let it go.
> ➤ Provide big picture.
> ➤ Support and encourage.
> ➤ Ask more than tell.
> ➤ Focus on the result...not on the nitty gritty process detail

you don't have to worry about burning bridges, if you're building your own"

— *Kerry E. Wagner*

Who gets ownership feelings?

> ➤ I get when I relate job performance with self image.
> ➤ I get when I Am passionate about my job.
> ➤ I get when I Understand excellence in job is well rewarded.
> ➤ I get when my organization is development oriented.

- ➢ I get when I Feel my responsibility is more than my contractual obligations.
- ➢ I get some time when I am closely obliged to a Boss.
- ➢ I get when my exceptional role in my life is recognized and appreciated.
- ➢ I get when I owe all my growth to my organization.
- ➢ I get when I know my colleagues are genuinely concerned of me.

PROFESSIONALISM

- ➢ Confidence in self/company/product/strategy.
- ➢ Integrity-consistency
- ➢ Expertise in job
- ➢ Credibility
- ➢ Planning the work-working plan
- ➢ Objective oriented-not subjective
- ➢ Decision making
- ➢ Managing time
- ➢ Perfectionist
- ➢ Consultant role
- ➢ Can repeat perform-demonstrate
- ➢ Accountability
- ➢ No compromise on self respect
- ➢ Communication skill-listening
- ➢ Presentation skill
- ➢ Positive perception
- ➢ Clear on objective-strategy-action –feedback
- ➢ Failures are for learning
- ➢ Clear and confident of results
- ➢ Perseverance

Skills

- ➢ Balance between results and means
- ➢ Visionary
- ➢ Leadership skills
- ➢ Trustworthy
- ➢ Priority to human relations
- ➢ Sober dress and appearance
- ➢ Optimum professional distance
- ➢ Focused on growth and profit
- ➢ Set and achieve time bound target
- ➢ Learn for vast knowledge
- ➢ Incorporate healthy service attitude

Professionalism is the epitome of managerial excellence ....

MASTERY OF COMMUNICATION SKILL

CONTENTS

Styles of communication (Formal and informal)

➢   How do you talk to your teacher?
➢   How do you talk to your Mother?
➢   How does a policeman talk to you?
➢   How does a doctor talk to you?
➢   How do you talk to your boss?
➢   How do you talk to your banker?
➢   How do you talk to your friend?

> How do you talk when you want to complain about a colleague?

> How do you behave when a stranger misbehaves with your sister on the road?

> How do you behave when a shopkeeper gives you a balance less than you are due?

> How do you behave while on a long distance train journey? Can you recollect the sequence of the conversation?

How can I be a Good communicator?

> Clear idea what I want to convey.

> Confidence on the relevant, subject, knowledge.

> Clarity in the steps sequence of my thought process.

> Use my chin tongue and lips to ensure clarity. What you say should be what he hears.

> Nonverbal language is a powerful tool in which there is appropriate use of body language.

> Maintain eye contact for observation and conveying subtle points.

> Ensure you are in focus and actively listening.

> Be assertive, not meek.

> Be open to other person's point of view.

> Response Vs Reaction is important.

> Give as much importance to communication as to listening.

"We are slaves of the spoken word and masters of the unspoken word"

"A man's character may be learned from the adjectives which he habitually uses in conversation."

Mark Twain

Guidelines for active listening

➤ Stop talking
➤ Show interest
➤ Listen to understand rather than oppose
➤ Remove distractions
➤ Be flexible
➤ Balance listening and speech speed
➤ Do not argue only to criticize
➤ Don't assume what he is saying
➤ Listen to content not the way he is delivering
➤ Put the speaker at ease
➤ Avoid distractions, phone calls, loud noise etc

"I consider conversations with people to be mind exercises, but I don't want to pull a muscle, so I stretch a lot. That's why I'm constantly either rolling my eyes or yawning."

— Jarod Kintz, It Occurred to Me

TELEPHONE MANNERS

➤ Identify yourself
➤ Be alert with body posture
➤ Use callers name frequently
➤ Inform the caller if you are holding transferring a call
➤ Apologize sincerely for customer inconvenience

> Adjust your response to feel positive while dealing with angry customers
> Watch speaking rate
> Incoming call, pickup within 2 rings

The marketing world is going round due to smart Telephone girls and there conversation skills......

Ten Commandments on telephone manners

> Pick up the phone as soon as possible, don't allow it to ring.
> Announce your name, she/he will have a feeling of commitment.
> Keep a smile on your face, she/he can feel it at the other end.
> Do not be unfriendly.
> Do not be inattentive.
> Do not be in a hurry.
> Do not hang up first.
> Do not be negative while passing information.
> Do not lose your cool.
> Be courteous even to the complaining customer.
> Tell him "we will sort it out".

The telephone, which interrupts the most serious conversations and cuts short the most weighty observations, has a romance of its own."
Virginia Woolf]

YOUR USP

SMILE
SHOW RESPECT
SHOW COURTESY
SHOW EMPATHY
AVOID CONTRAVERSY
AGREE TO DISAGREE

"You are your greatest asset. Put your time, effort and money into training grooming, and encouraging your greatest asset."-Tom Hopkins

ETIQUETE

BE POLITE
BE PUNCTUAL
DONT SHOW OR LOOSE TEMPER
DONT POINT AT OTHERS
REMOVE HAT INDOORS
DELIVER A GOOD HAND SHAKE
SAY PLEASE AND THANK YOU OFTEN
OPEN DOORS FOR OTHERS
ALWAYS GREET SOMEONE WHEN THEY COME HOME
WAIT FOR SOMETIME AND DONT INTERRUPT OTHER PEOPLE
KEEP CELLPHONE IN SILENT MODE DURING A MEETING
KEEP TO THE RIGHT SIDE WHILE WALK ING ON THE STAIR CASE

KEEP FOOD, FOLDER ETC ON YOUR LEFT HAND

YOUR RIGHT SHOULD BE FREE FOR HAND SHAKE

DO NOT WALK AND HAND SHAKE

MAKE EYE CONTACT

SHAKE HAND ONLY ONCE OR TWICE NOT MORE

ALWAYS RESPECT ALL ELDERS LISTEN AND LEARN

ASK FOR CLARIFICATIONS PROPERLY

CHECK YOUR VOICE FOR CHARACTER AND PERSONALITY

MAKE MEANINGFUL INTERRUPTION

PROJECT A POSITIVE, MATURE PERSONALITY

GROUP DISCUSSION

Group Discussion today is a very common tool for personality testing. It enables the HR Manager to judge the candidates communication skills, Initiative and leadership. Your confidence level and attitude is also assessed.

1) **Procedure for GD**

- ✓ Selection of number of candidates.
- ✓ Assignment of serial number.
- ✓ Announcing the topic.
- ✓ Initiation of Discussion.
- ✓ Logical points of view.
- ✓ Watch for arguments.
- ✓ Overall Behavior.
- ✓ Conclusion.

2) **Expectation of HR Manager**

3) **Topics for GD**

- Pot Holes in Cochin Roads
- Women Empowerment
- Our Educational System
- Employability
- Why English Fluency
- Why Positive Attitude
- Mind, My Master
- Role of Sports in overall Education
- Why Unemployment
- Up's and Down's of aviation Industry
- Customer Relation's
- Global Warming
- Aviation Industry- Crisis & Solution
- Democracy – Will it Survive
- Adhar Identity, Importance
- Indo –Pak Relations
- Anna Hazare
- Banking Boom
- Food Bill
- Are Women Unsafe in India
- Are Political Parties a hindrance to Development
- CSR of MNC'S
- Kerala Politics
- Media Sensationalizing
- Freedom of Expression
- Obesity- Solutions
- Financial Crisis- Global
- Crashing of Indian Rupee
- Solar Issue

- ➢ Tourism – Potential
- ➢ Digital – Traditional Advertisement
- ➢ New Generation Cinema's – Ethics &Content
- ➢ Face Book – Boom or Doom
- ➢ Capital Punishment for Rapists.
- ➢ Media Power
- ➢ Use and Misuse of Mobile Phones

4) <u>**Expectations of the Company from the Candidate**</u>

a) Confidence
b) Communication Skill
c) Listening Skill
d) Active Listening
e) Patience
f) Respond and not React
g) English Fluency
h) Note down the names of the members
i) Flexibility
j) Sense of humour
k) Learning Attitude

I Take Charge of My Life

Now
Why?
That will Change my Life
Change What?
My Quality of Life
Yes, And Also My Environment and
My Country

YES! WE CAN.
50% of India's Population is like me
Between 18 and 25
Our minds are second to none
I don't expect anything from any body
My Intention
My Learning attitude
My Energy
My Confidence

Your life is what you make of it. It does not depend on anything else in the world

YES! WE WILL CHANGE;

PROSPERITY AND PEACE

IS

JUST AHEAD OF US

Yes, change happens only, if you

vote

ACKNOWLEDGEMENTS

To my wife Kothai who always helped me to learn.
To my children Kannamma, and Duddu, who are my eyes.
To my grand children Chiku and Gundu
who show me what is love.
To my many friends who helped me to think I can.
To my many students and friends who helped me
with the drafting, reading, spell check, editing
and finally approving this final copy.
This is a dream fulfilled for me which would
don't have been possible without reading the
many excellent books, magazines etc.
For me these cover what I know is the Al mighty

Dr. Rabindranath Athri
Shobanjali, Chilavannur road,
Kadavanthara, Cochin-682020
Mob-9995449763
athri.mentor@gmail.com

SOFT SKILL TRAINER

Developing soft skills in colleges, final year school children and corporates has been my passion for 17 years. My 44 modules reflect experience, range of topics and various industries.

- Self Actualisation
- Role Play
- Self Esteem
- Total Quality Individual

NLP TRAINER

NLP is a powerful subjective inward journey exercise by observing others with respect to communications, Body language, behavioral patterns, audio, visual&kinesthetic.

I have been doing this programme since 1991 in over 55 companies and institutions apart from training MBA student of ICFAI in Kerala &Tamil-Nadu (1200 Students).

Case Studies

Cochin International Airport LTD

Achieved Mindset Change during a 3 day program

- ❖ English fluency for midrange executives
- ❖ Induction program for new recruits
- ❖ Development of managerial expertise for "To be managers"

- Recognizing opportunity
- Confidence
- Positive attitude
- Stress management